THE 2016 ELECTION COLLECTOR'S EDITION

Trump for Principal:
A Children's Book for American Grownups

&

Secret Agent Hillary
and the Case of the Missing Hotdog

Written by Beth Schaefer
Illustrated by Hasby Mubarok

Trump for Principal. This book is dedicated to David. Our friendship is rich, and our laughs are priceless.

Secret Agent Hillary. This book is dedicated to my kickass, powerhouse nieces: Sadie and Madeline.

TABLE OF CONTENTS

Trump for Principal * (pages 3-26)
Secret Agent Hillary ** (pages 27-46)
Notes & Bios & Books (pages 47-50)

GENRES DEFINED

* <u>Political Satire:</u> A significant part of satire that specializes in gaining entertainment from politics. Political satire is usually distinguished from political protest or political dissent, as it does not necessarily carry an agenda nor seek to influence the political process. While occasionally it may, it more commonly aims simply to provide entertainment. By its very nature, it rarely offers a constructive view in itself; when it is used as part of protest or dissent, it tends to simply establish the error of matters rather than provide solutions.

**<u>Absurdist Fiction:</u> A genre that focuses on the experiences of characters in situations where they cannot find any inherent purpose in life, most often represented by ultimately meaningless actions and events that call into question the certainty of existential concepts such as truth or value. Common elements in absurdist fiction include satire, dark humor, incongruity, the abasement of reason, and controversy regarding the philosophical condition of being "nothing."

PUBLISHED BY:

Books on a Whim (Evanston)
Copyright 2015-16 (2016 Edition)
All Rights Reserved
ISBN: 978-0-578-17052-7
BooksOnAWhim.com

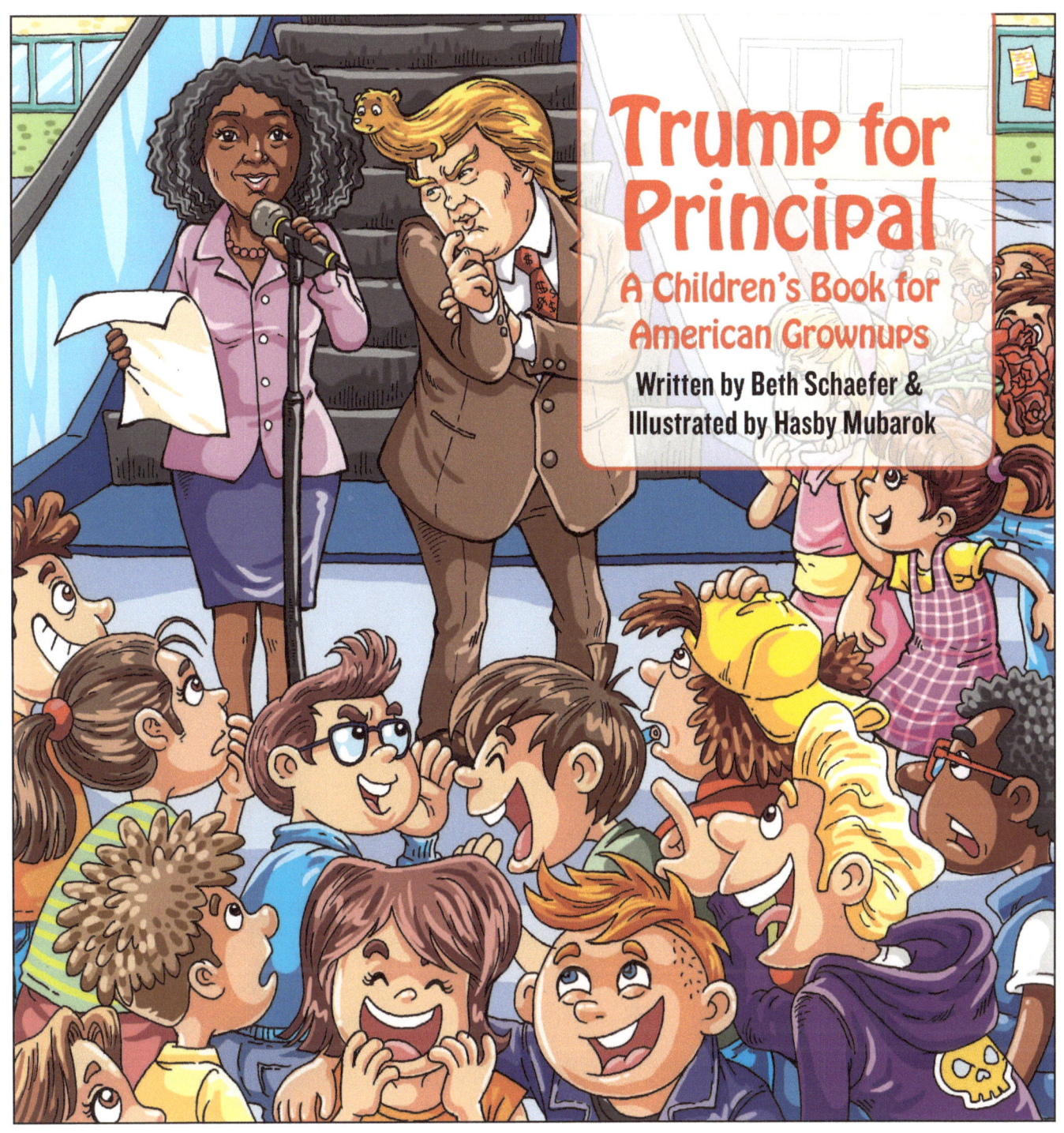

Trump for Principal:
A Children's Book for American Grownups

We are all sad to see Principal Moss go. She is sooooo nice and she loves kids. Me (my name's Jewel) and my class get to eat lunch with her when we get 15 Gold Stars for good manners.

Principal Moss is retiring because she's old. She wants to see Paris, but can't because she's got no money. But she says going to the Wisconsin Dells is just as good. She even goes down waterslides even though she's old! I hope Principal Moss will go to Paris before she dies.

Daddy says Principal Moss was pretty before her hairs went gray. Mommy gets mad when Daddy says Principal Moss was pretty, but she laughs when he says her hairs went gray.

When I retire I will be rich. Mommy says I'm so smart I can be President if I put my mind to it.

We are all wondering who is going to be our New Principal.

We ask Miss Bailey, and she says lots of grownups are intervuwding (that means fighting) to take Principal Moss's job. Lincoln School has a rule that kids can't fight.

I think our New Principal will be young and pretty. She'll have golden flowy hair like a Princess. And she will always be smiling and happy because she loves kids.

She will wear pink puffy dresses and at Halloween she will sprinkle glitter in her golden flowy hair like a Fairy.

When we get 15 Gold Stars she will give us pieces of chocolate cake.
Her name will be Ariel. I can't WAIT to see her!

The New Principal is COMING AFTER RECESS! We can't wait!!!!!! We can't wait!!!!!!

Gracie says she will throw roses at her...Ariel...like at Miss America, but Miss Bailey says, "Put those roses back in your locker. They're dangerous."
I think so too. We don't want to stick thorns in Ariel's skin.

When the bell rings, we go inside. Teachers tell us to wait at the bottom of the escalator.
There are zillions of us. Our halls don't have air conditioners, so it smells stinky.

I'm a good runner because I run good fast.
I'm so close to the escalator I can almost touch it.
It's moving!! It's moving!! There she is…! She's…

…a man???

Well, he seems really friendly.
He smiles super big and has a pet weasel on his head. That's nice!

Ooooooh, I like his necktie with the swirls.
Daddy says neckties are for losers who want to look like winners.
But I like neckties. They look like princess ribbons.

Shhhhhhh.....Old Principal Moss is going to say something....

"Kids, I introduce Lincoln School's new chief, Principal Trump. He will make Lincoln great again! Principal Trump will be making many changes. His first change is our school mission: **HOPE. CHANGE. FORWARD** to **FORWARD STEADY CHARGE**. Let's give Principal Trump a warm Lincoln welcome!"

I'm so excited! I'm so excited! We all clap and Gracie throws her roses anyway.

Oh, my God! Oh, my God! He's going to talk! Here he goes....

$Everything in life is luck.$
Neat! His voice is scratchy like a billygoat.

$Well, I ran for Principal as a Republican. I have a lot of confidence in the Republican Party, unlike they in me. But like them, I don't have a lot of confidence in this Principal.$
Principal Trump points at Old Principal Moss.

$I think what is happening to this school is unbelievably bad. We're no longer a respected school.$ Huh? Why is Old Principal Moss running away crying? What's he saying to Miss Missy?

$It's time Lincoln School was run like a business. I just love real estate.$
I love houses! I will live in a house when I'm rich. I think I'm going to like Principal Trump....

But he doesn't give high-fives.

"I think that the only thing better than a good high-five is no high-five at all. I've long said high-fives are a bad idea because of all the germs people spread when they high-five. I think the high-five is barbaric. Giving high-fives, you catch the flu, you catch this, you catch all sorts of things," Principal Trump says.

It's 2 weeks now Principal Trump is at Lincoln.

Principal Moss's office looks really different now.

Something peculiar is happening in Room 110. Juanita and Gabriela and José stopped showing up.

Maybe they're home sick, but that's a really long time. And they're getting behind on learning about plants. Juanita and Gabriela and José are super hard workers. They never miss school.

I ask Miss Bailey where they are, but she turns white. I think she misses them too.

Specially, I miss Juanita. Her and me dress up like twins every Halloween hall parade.

I'm getting kind of scared I might disappear too .....

And my other friend too's gone, a grownup. Mr. John the custodian. He's missing. We ALL miss Mr. John. He's super silly.

Once Mr. John went inside the janitor's closet and shut the door. He played prisoner and me and my friends played sheriffs.

When we let him out, Mr. John was laughing so hard he fell to the floor! He said he peed from laughing, but would mop it up. We all knew it was just water from the drinking fountain.

We miss our Mr. John games. Plus the floors are getting messy.

Sometimes Principal Trump plays with us.

He picks on us, but we never get a chance to run.

Lincoln has computers in the library that we learn on about the earth and dinosores and things. Miss Nicole the librarian shows us where the keys go, but she went gone too.

Principal Trump makes us type letters that don't make words. They make faces come up. I type with one finger. It takes so long it hurts. But Principal Trump wants more.

$There should be a lot of systems. Beyond databases. I mean, Lincoln School should have a lot of systems. We're going to have to look at a lot of things very closely.$ He said something about looking at mosqueitos, so I think next we'll learn about insects like butterflys.

Once Principal Trump got so mad at a girl who came up on my computer that he hacked it. $I could see there was blood coming out of her eyes. Blood coming out of her wherever.$ I didn't see the blood, but the glass cut Henry's finger.

16

WINTER BREAK is almost here! Principal Trump says there will be a HOLIDAY PARTY in the gym! I love parties! There will be cupcakes, balloons, pony rides, Simon Says, lemonade too!

Santa will come! I'll sit on his lap and say what I want that I won't get like the Fairy Princess Castle.

I go to the gym and hear creepy music like scratchy wires. Oh my....there are buttlers. And there are tablecloths on our lunch tables. And foods like baby goldfishs and teeny tiny wieners. Eewww!

Principal Trump has the school nurse, Miss Lexie, on his lap, but he isn't dressed like Santa. Oh, well. At least they had a clown.

New Years is here. Principal Trump shouts at us over the loud speaker. That's where we used to sing "I Pledge Allegiance." We don't sing anymore, we obey.

$I learn from the past, but plan for the future by focusing on the present. There's where the fun is.$ I don't really get that part.

$The point is that you can't be too greedy.$ That part I get. Sometimes I'm greedy when I steal cookies from the Milton's house next door. Now I know that's ok.

Principal Trump speaks really loud.

Principal Trump says it's a new fineanchul year. So we must reorganize. I agree. My desk is a mess. My crayons are all mixed up in sandwitch bags with my markers.

He is calling grownups to his office. Not real teachers like Miss Bailey. He is calling *not not not* real teachers like Miss Susie my speech teacher, Miss Bob from PE, Miss Lexie the nurse, Miss Meadows the music teacher, and Mr. Carney the school social worker.

Sally just came from bathroom break with her hall pass and she says she saw them. Sally says one-at-a-time the *not not not* real teachers are going into the Principal's Office and coming out with cardboard boxes.

Lately, I'm having trouble again with my "th's" and I'm getting shaky again during tornado drills. I can still lie in the nurse's cot, but nobody feels my forehead.

Principal Trump makes Mommy mad. I overhear her telling Daddy. Daddy's a good lissener. Tonight she went to parent/teacher conferences, and now she's back home. Principal Trump told Mommy her pants were too tight and that she should take her pants off or go on a diet.

Mommy says "disgusting pig" to Daddy. But she's not talking about Daddy.
But I can't figure out if she is calling Principal Trump a "disgusting pig,"
or if Principal Trump called Mommy a $disgusting pig.$

Grownups are terribly confusing.
Who is the good guy? Who is the bad guy?
Should I love Principal Trump? Or should I hate him?

I've decided to HATE Principal Trump.

He embarrassed me in front of most of the whole school. I have a special ticket for free lunches. I get free lunches since Daddy lost his job and Mommy's waitressing. Daddy says I get a special ticket because I'm special.

It is almost my turn in the lunchline for chicken nuggets. Ummm…Principal Trump is studying my ticket. Miss Chin, the lunch lady, tells him "Jewel's ticket gets her free lunch."

Principal Trump says: $A certificate of free lunch is not the same thing by any stretch of the imagination as a free lunch certificate. $ ALL my friends hear him. He takes my special ticket away from me. I'm soooo hungry so Miss Chin sneaks me some nuggets. She's really nice. Principal Trump says Miss Chin has to stay for affirmuhtive action. That means war, I think.

Since Principal Trump moved the climbing walls from the gym to the soccer feeled, recess is a little scary. The PTA parents are showing up on the grass.

Principal Trump's frends are showing up too. They're throwing food. I don't think all this food should be wasted by throwing it away or at the PTA.

$They put the wrong fingers in the air. I'd like to punch them in the face.$ Principal Trump yells at moms and dads. $Do you know what used to happen to parents like that when they were in a place like this? They'd be carried out on a stretcher, folks.$

Everybody's running around. But I'm too tired.

The Friday before Memorial Day, Principal Trump holds an assembly. I'm in the second row. Since I don't have PE anymore I'm not as fast.

Principal Trump's voted himself Mr. America cause he says we don't have brains enough to vote. That's why we're here. That's why we're in school.

He's going to give a acceptance speech. Hmm, maybe it'll be nice.
 $Experience taught me to listen to your gut. The second is that you're better off sticking with what you know. And the third is sometimes your best investments are the ones you don't make.$

He sounds smart. Smarter than me. Maybe he's not so bad after all.

School just let out for SUMMER BREAK!!!!

As I'm walking home from school, I'm thinking ....A lot has changed since Principal Trump was elected. My friends are gone, the halls are messy, my lisp is back, Mommy's mad, and I'm hungry.

Still. Today Principal Trump announced that Lincoln will have some schoolyard improvedmints made over the summer. I think it's a new tireswing since ours is moldy....and a shiny new jungle gym with monkey bars that don't snap off.

...Hmm, I suppose Principal Trump deserves a second chance.

True, Second Grade was kind of rough.
But Third Grade is going to be my BEST YEAR YET!!!!!

THE END

Actual Trump Quotes:

"Sadly the American dream is dead," Trump declared upon descending on an escalator in the Trump Tower on 5th Avenue to announce his 2016 presidential candidacy.

"Everything in life is luck."

"Well, I am a Republican, and I would run (for president) as a Republican. And I have a lot of confidence in the Republican Party. I don't have a lot of confidence in the president. I think what is happening to this country is unbelievably bad. We're no longer a respected country."

"Perhaps it's time America was run like a business. I just love real estate."

"I think that the only thing better than a good handshake is no handshake at all. I've long said handshakes are a bad idea because of all the germs people spread when they shake hands. I think the handshake is barbaric ...I wouldn't mind a little bow."

"I've never had a glass of alcohol. I won't even drink a cup of coffee."

"I try to learn from the past, but I plan for the future by focusing on the present. There's where the fun is."... "The point is that you can't be too greedy."

"We're going to have to look at a lot of things very closely. We're going to have to look at the mosques. We're going to have to look very, very carefully."

"There should be a lot of systems (that track Muslims in the country) Beyond databases. I mean, we should have a lot of systems."

"You could see there was blood coming out of her eyes. Blood coming out of her wherever." (Referring to debate moderator Megyn Kelly.)

"They walk in and they put their hand up and they put the wrong finger in the air ... and they get away with murder. Because we've become weak."

"I'd like to punch him in the face, I tell ya. You know what they used to do to guys like that when they were in a place like this? They'd be carried out on a stretcher, folks."

"Does everybody know Rosie O'Donnell? She's a disgusting pig, right?"

"A certificate of live birth is not the same thing by any stretch of the imagination as a birth certificate."

"Experience taught me a few things. One is listen to your gut. The second is that you're better off sticking with what you know. And the third is sometimes your best investments are the ones you don't make."

"Miss Universe criticized me for telling the truth about illegal immigration, but then said she would keep the crown. Idiot."

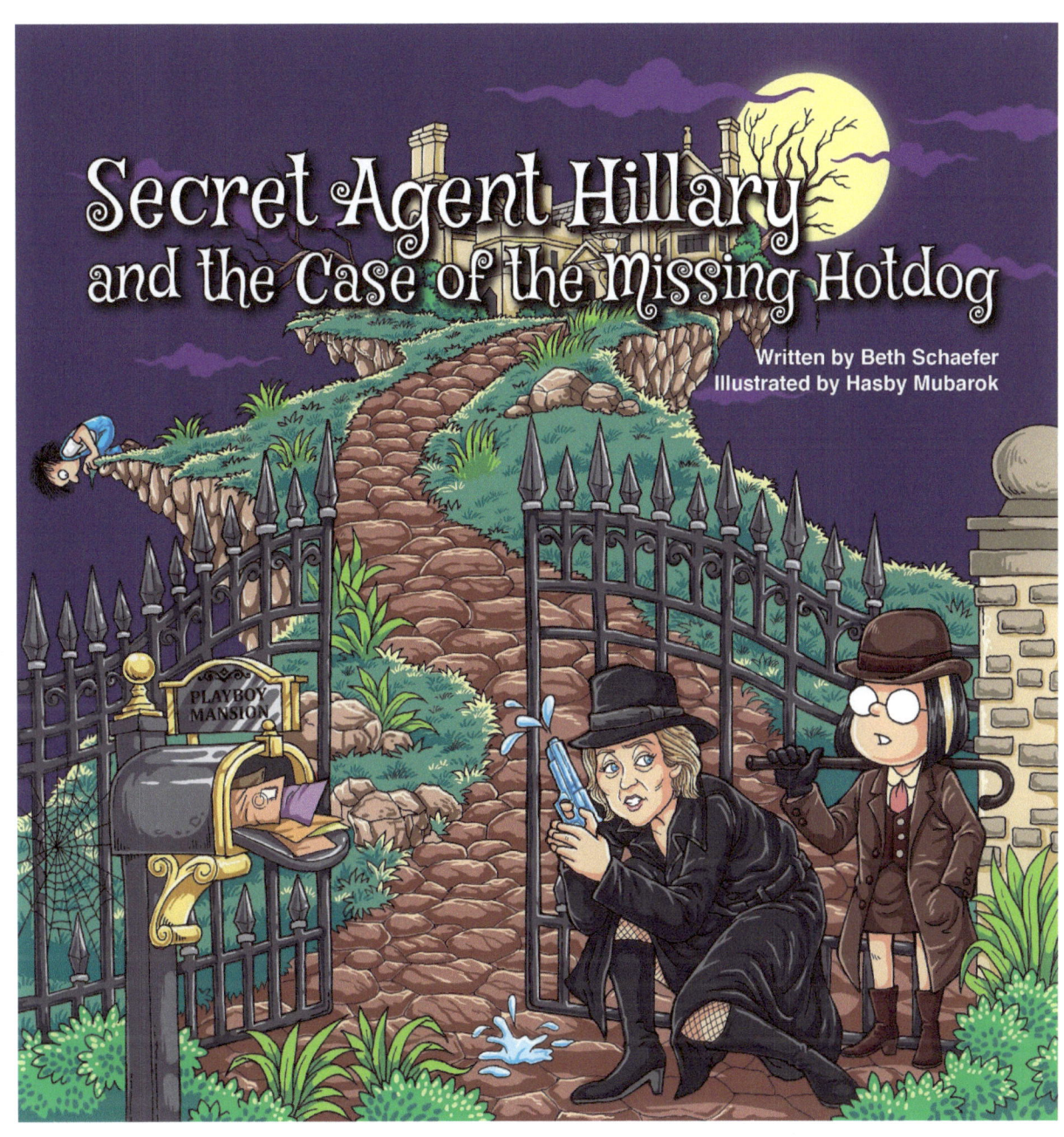

Secret Agent Hillary and the Case of the Missing Hotdog
and the Case of the Missing Hotdog

Hillary loved being Senior Sergeant. She loved catching criminals. She loved saving lives. She loved working with Assistant Sergeant Macy.

But she longed to be an investigator. You see, Hillary had more than brawn, she had brains.

One summer night, Hillary's fate changed. She tracked down Wally the pickpocket, a terribly difficult man to find.

And Hillary's wish came true.

The day Hillary was promoted to Secret Agent was the happiest day of her life.

She was so happy, she was happier than the time she made history as the first female valedictorian to recite Newton.

She was so happy, she was happier than the time Billy the Cook counter proposed.

She was even happier than the time she won Secretary of Skate.

Hillary's first assignment was a hard one. Her new boss had given her a tough nut to crack.

It was the case of the missing hotdog.

The hotdog belonged to Hugh Heffner, Curator of the Playboy Mansion in Los Angeles.

On-site survellience cameras first misled them to think they had caught the culprit hiding the goods in his pants.

But upon further inspection, the privates realized the crook was still at large.

Hillary and Macy, who was now Secret Sidekick, scoped out the mansion's lay of the land.

Was the thief still on the premises? Did the thief escape? Did the thief leave any clues at the gate?

Hillary and Macy came up with nothing, and they approached the mansion to meet the Curator himself.

"I knew this was no matter for the police," Hugh Heffner said. "I needed private eyes because everyone and everything here goes down in secret."

"Tell us about the hotdog," Hillary ordered.

"Gladly," Hugh said. "I bought that hotdog at a cart in Beverly Hills. It was the biggest, most beautiful hotdog I had ever seen."

"I paid the vendor its worth," he continued. "$10,000."

Hugh took a puff from his pipe. "But it's not the hotdog's monetary value I miss. It's its sentimental value. See, the hotdog compensates for my personal shortcomings."

"Show me the scene of the crime," said Hillary.

"Follow me," said Hugh, and he led the two privates through a swinging party to reach his gallery.

"Who are these guests?" Hillary asked.

"On top of the bunnies, mostly celebrities," Hugh replied. "I only invite famous people to my parties."

"Interesting…" thought Hillary.

When they reached the gallery, Hugh showed Hillary a giant empty bun.

"Hmmm," said Hillary. "When did you last see the hotdog?"

"It was with me this morning when I woke up," Hugh told her.

Hillary observed the display case. "No broken glass. No fingerprints. No code or lock."

"That's correct," Hugh responded. "Our thief must be very agile."

"Look there!" Hillary exclaimed. "The painting on the wall!"

She led Macy to a giant painting of swirls and strokes.

"Why, this painting is splattered." Macy observed.

"Exactly!" declared Hillary. "Relish. Mustard. Diced onions. Ketchup. Sauerkraut. Chili. These are exactly the clues we are looking for!"

"If we find the source of the condiments, we find the thief." Hillary turned to Hugh. "Which guests left tonight's party early?" Hugh gave her six names.

Case Report

Suspect 1: Bernie Bathers
Condiment in question: The Relish
Operation: The private eyes entered suspect's house. There they proceeded secretly to the bathroom, following the sound of running water and singing.

Upon secret entry, they saw suspect in the bath, scrubbing his back with relish.

It appears suspect mixes relish with his bath salt.

CONCLUSION:

Case Report - continued

Suspect 2: Donald Trumpf
Condiment in question: The Mustard
Operation: The private eyes located suspect at the Bully Fight Saloon. Privates secretly cased the bar to find Sammy the Tender, Meggy the Moderator, and suspect himself riding a mechanical golden elephant.

It was concluded the suspect was using the mustard to squirt gold colored glop as a riding lubricant.

CONCLUSION:

Case Report - continued

Suspect 3: Sarah Pallin
Condiment in question: Diced Onions
Operation: The private eyes located suspect on a platform. Suspect was on the path to execute a turkey.

Suspect was throwing diced onions at turkey bystanders. Suspect seemed to be using onions for a tear jerk effect.

CONCLUSION:

Case Report - continued

Suspect 4: Chris Crissy
Condiment in question: The Ketchup
Operation: The private eyes tracked down suspect in his playroom. Suspect was playing cars on his train table.

Suspect used ketchup as toy blood which was all over his cars and his hands.

CONCLUSION:

Case Report - continued

Suspect 5: Arnold Schwarzenagger
Condiment in question: The Sauerkraut
Operation: Secret Agent decided to try a new technique, which was to disguise herself and approach suspect directly. Agent disguised herself as reporter.

Agent interrogated suspect at his office. Agent learned that suspect does not eat sauerkraut as a topping. It was determined suspect eats sauerkraut as finger food.

CONCLUSION:

Case Report - continued

Suspect 6: Bengassi Committee
Condiment in question: The Chili
Operation: Secret Agent crashed suspect's dinner in a game of cat and mouse. With no choice but to play along, Agent sat for supper. As the meal wore on, Agent held her breath for something telling to transpire.

But in the end, Agent concluded suspect consumed chili for the sake of gas alone.

CONCLUSION:

"That clears our six suspects," Hillary said.
"Should we go home?" Macy asked.

Hillary snapped her fingers. "Wait! I've got it! What if we've been looking for the wrong topping. In fact, what if the clue we're looking for isn't a topping at all. Macy, follow me!"

Hillary led Macy to the Dog n Suds. "It was right before our eyes the whole time. Macy, where do hotdog thieves hide themselves?"
"Why, among other hotdog lovers," Macy exclaimed.

"Exactly! And what do hotdog lovers drink?" Hillary answered her own question. "Beer, of course! And the missing hotdog is huge! So, whoever has drunk the most beer at Dog n Suds is our man! And there she is. Elizabeth Warden, I should have known. You're under arrest for stealing a hotdog."

CASE CLOSED

That night after the commotion, Hillary walked home.

Her first case was a success. Warden was behind bars. Her boss was happy. Hugh had closure.

It started to drizzle.

"I've done good," Hillary told herself. She knew Secret Agent was the job for her.

Hillary yawned, "Tonight I will sleep a long deep sleep. I have to."

"Because tomorrow," she thought, "it's the case of the missing umbrella."

NOTES FROM AUTHOR

TRUE STORY: In 1998, **Hillary Clinton** appeared at the Concourse Hotel in Madison, Wisconsin to endorse Senator **Russ Feingold** in his '98 campaign. There was a torrential downpour and Hillary's secret service men were ill-prepared; they needed an umbrella to hold over the first lady as they ushered her in. I was at the hotel to hear her speak, and I loaned them my umbrella. I was excited to get my umbrella back so I could keep it forever and tell its story. Unfortunately, Hillary's secret service never gave me back my umbrella.

TREASURED DAY: On November 10, 2015, my son **Tony** and I stood outside Chicago's Trump Tower to hawk my first edition of Trump for Principal. With his teacher's blessing, I took Tony out of school that day, and for four hours we stood on the Michigan Avenue Bridge, held up our banners, and shouted at the top of our lungs "Trump for Principal, not President." I was so proud of Tony for running up to the hundreds of passersby (it was during lunch hour) and handing out flyers, telling complete strangers: "Trump for Principal, not President." Tony, you're the bestest!

Principal Moss in Paris: Merci to FUSAC Magazine for bringing Principal Moss to Paris. C'est très agréable que vous fassiez ses rêves se matérialiser.

ABOUT THE AUTHOR:

Beth Schaefer started writing comedy in 2013 at the age of 38. She founded her publishing company Books on a Whim that same year. Beth's books are primarily humor, but she is also branching into family-centered, educational, and social issue-related genres.

ABOUT THE ILLUSTRATOR:

Hasby Mubarok has been drawing since he was a child. He graduated with a degree in Visual Design at the Indonesian Institute of Art. At 30-years-old (2016), Hasby is an up-and-coming artist in Indonesia, who often exhibits at art expos. Look out for his first comic strip "Madura dalam Canda!"

IN APPRECIATION:
"Dear Hasby, I am incredibly lucky that our paths have crossed. Thank you for your invaluable contribution to these two books. You are an outstanding artist and I am happy to know you. (Hopefully someday we'll actually meet.) Keren selama-lamanya!"

- Beth

The Nutty Years of the Jon Stewart Presidency in a Nutshell
This mock term paper pokes wacky fun across party lines and at a slew of celebrities. Jon Stewart is elected U.S. President. And boy is it one crazy term! Beth Schaefer's satirical story contains wordplay, innuendos, celebrity and politician scandals, and spoofs of all sorts of controversies. If you like lots of words, wit, U.S. history, edge, pop culture, and absurdity, this is the book for you. Rated R.

Sometimes I wish I had a dad (and an Xbox)
This richly illustrated book is customized for children (ages 4-9) who have absent dads. This book portrays a loving variety of kind, paternal men—in the form of teacher, uncle, coach, neighbor, and more. This book celebrates the people who are present in a child's life, demonstrating the joy life still affords despite a parent's abandonment. Rated G.

Grade A Papers: A funny coffee table book for English teachers and the universe
This collection of funny, refreshingly original fake student papers is stocked with custom-made art on nearly every paper. This book pokes friendly fun at the random eccentricities and idiosyncrasies of college teachers and students. Rated PG-13.

Coming soon:
Grade A Papers II: A funny coffee table book for history teachers and the universe
Welcome to the world of Whimsor College. Whimsor is a fictional liberal arts college located in Columbia, Missouri, just north of Shady Lake and east of Bear Creek Trail. Like its predecessor, this collection of quirky fake student papers is rich with custom-made art on nearly every paper. Rated PG.

Support Artists,
Not Giants.
Bookstore:
www.booksonawhim.com

Books on a Whim

Visit: BooksOnAWhim.com
Email: info@BooksOnAWhim.com
Write: Books on a Whim
PO Box 5066,
Evanston, IL 60204-5066

www.ingramcontent.com/pod-product-compliance
Lightning Source LLC
Chambersburg PA
CBHW041523220426
43669CB00002B/34